Public Speaking Tips & Quips 2:

Beyond the Fear

Preface

As a public speaking educator for over 13 years, I've had the chance to observe many speakers struggle with planning the structure and outline of a speech, not because they are not knowledgeable. Learning how to organize our thoughts is not easy. It's a gradual process. If you take it in strides, you can prepare an effective outline for a speech.

This short book on public speaking will provide you with tools to choose a topic, plan for the event, and analyze your audience to increase your chances of successfully wooing your listeners.

"A good speech is like a pencil; it has to have a point." Author unknown

I'm confused? Where do I begin?

You have a 5-7 minute speech to give, and you're not sure where to start. What am I supposed to say? What should I talk about?

Let's get right to it.

First, you need a topic. This is a broad area of general interest or expertise.

- Example 1: Communication
- Example 2: Health

However, a topic is too broad. You could take a million directions when deciding where to go with your topic, but you can't follow all of them in a fairly short speech. So, you need to be a little choosy.

A subject or narrow focus related to your topic would be easier to plan, since it is simply a little slice of a topic, rather than the whole tostada.

For example, communication is a general topic you can further break down into many subtopics or subjects. Health is another general area of interest you can narrow to a specific subject.

- Example 1: Communication – Business Communication – Customer Service
- Example 2: Health – Professions – Nursing – Gerontology/Geriatrics

It is simpler to plan a speech when your focus is narrow and specific. Why?

Research is better targeted to information you will need to address the needs, goals, and wants of the intended audience attending the specific speaking event.

You can strip your subject to the key points relevant to your speech focus. The end game is an easier method of planning your points and learning the information.

This lessens the chance you will feel overwhelmed when you are deciding how much information you should include without overloading yourself or listeners with too many unnecessary details.

Next, choose your intent. You can give a million speeches on any subject, but all the information would not fit cozily within a 5 minute speech slot.

To make your speech prep easier, you need some pointers on **who, what, when, where, why,** and **how** for the specific talk, seminar, or event.

Scenario 1: Who are you? (Role or position) – Communication Consultant

- Who is the audience? – CSR Reps, Small Business Office
- What is the stated goal? – Customer Service Training
- What is your instructional goal? – Inform and Motivate
- What is the professional goal? – Gain additional experience as consultant
- What is the listener's level? – Beginner
- When are you giving the speech? – Next week
- Where are you giving the speech? – Office, conference room
- Why are you giving the speech? – Job skills training
- How often have you spoken to this group? - Never

Scenario 2: Who are you? (Role or Position) – Nurse Educator

- Who is the audience? – Geriatric Nurses
- What is the stated goal? – Continued Education
- What is the professional goal? – Demonstrate capacity to manage nursing staff
- What is the corporate goal? – Inform and Enforce Policy
- What is the listener's level? – Advanced/Expert
- When are you giving the speech? – Next month
- Where are you giving the speech? – Away, Conference room
- Why are you giving the speech? – Continuing Education
- How often have you spoken to this group? – Often, weekly

Quite a few questions. Yes, they are many but important. If you go through this process of understanding who, what, when, where, why and how, you will be better prepared to face your audience with strategies tailored to their needs, goals, and interests. You will also feel more confident entering new or unfamiliar speaking situations.

The next step is to determine the value or benefit you expect listeners will take away from the experience of listening to your speech. In English Composition, Writing or Speech courses, this is called the thesis statement.

However, since we are not in a classroom, you want a word which fits what you are trying to accomplish with your speech or presentation: the value or benefit to the listener. Why should they listen? They want reasons why they should give you their time. What will make them want to listen? What's their motivation or incentive?

By listening, we are speaking of the full body experience of watching, engaging, enlightening, and retaining (WEER). So, what do you want to do to your listeners? In this case, you want to "WEER them out".

In planning for your listeners, here are a few questions to consider:

- What have you given them to look at?
- What are you doing to make them curious and receptive?
- How can you make them feel the need and want to have the knowledge you have?

Now, why the word "**knowledge**" and not "information"? Knowledge is appreciated for its value to those who seek or stumble across it especially if you surprise your listeners with unexpected insights.

On the other hand, **information** may be random details or lists of unrelated facts and figures with no thought behind their combination except to drown us in a sea of flotsam and jetsam.

Every day we are bombarded with so much data, that it's almost a full time job to make sense of it all. We need someone to take away the burden of wading through all the information drowning our focus, and make sense of it.

So, we appreciate when someone can break it down all that seemingly endless and random data for us into short, simple, and easy to understand information.

First, we identify the knowledge buried in the information. Knowledge has reason and value. It also contains a purpose and frame.

Information is limitless but our individual knowledge is finite. Yes, there is an end. With knowledge, we can choose many destinations, but consequently, all must move towards a desired outcome or endgame.

This result is derived from all the combined effort you're investing to make the speech a success for the amount of time you are given to make a ripple.

A speech without an endgame is like a wanderer in a maze. You're walking aimlessly, bumping into dead ends, and you're crossing your fingers hoping the person behind you is patient enough to stay with you despite your uncertain direction.

Listeners will only follow you so far before they lose interest.

How do you show you're in charge of the endgame? First, value the listener's attention. They may nor may not have paid to hear you speak. Respect that time and willingness to give you some undivided attention.

Next, get their interest. Value is perceived, received, and believed. It is the conscious and shown appreciation for your listeners' time and potential interest in the attitude, approach, and attention you give to speech planning, preparation, and presentation.

"Your purpose is to make your audience see what you saw; hear what you heard, feel what you felt." – Dale Carnegie

Potential interest is your ability to inspire listeners to be open and see possible benefits or value in your message despite initial reservations or disinterest. How will you appeal to their need to feel wanted, understood, interested, and connected?

If you approach your speech assuming failure because you think there is no way you can enliven them enough to get your message across, then your body language will likely reflect that you gave up although the presentation has barely begun.

Does this mean, you will feel convincingly ready to make them listen at the start? Not necessarily. There's always a few stray nerves or two to rattle us a little. We can handle it, right? (You know, we got this)

So, should you suddenly assume a feeling of complete and self-assured confidence regardless of any concerns or insecurities?

No, since this would place too much pressure on your already nervous psyche. It would also encourage you to have too many high expectations for yourself, leading to unrealistic goals, and later on, disappointment if you don't achieve them exactly as you expected.

Feelings of extreme disappointment will not help fraying nerves. They could leave you feeling less hopeful or inspired for the next speech. Similar to the worry many will have when they've done something well, you may feel pressure to repeat that success at the cost of self-confidence.

No one wants to place themselves in a situation where they feel discomfort about a job not done well. When we enter a new situation, we focus on self-protection and self-preservation. We are not going to readily place ourselves in a position where we feel powerless.

Living on either sides of the complete success or failure divide is not helpful.

- The first, complete success, gives you little room to make mistakes and grow, and
- The second, complete failure, gives you little room to feel positive about your

chances of being successful or seeing progress or growth in the future.

Don't try to take on the world or knock the ball out of the park with the first speech. (Same rule applies if you're a writer). Start with simple goals and expectations.

Goals are planned from your **perspective** as the speaker or presenter, and **expectations** are approached from the listener's perspective. Both are two sides of the same coin. The question is how to make the two **meet, marry,** and **meringue**.

Whet the listener's appetite.

Start by getting to know your listener. What kinds of subjects or experiences are important or interesting to the ones who wait expectantly for that juicy morsel you saved for them?

- What sparks their interests or makes the world appealing to them?
- Why are these interests appealing?
- How can you turn that curiosity into something they will want to follow down the rabbit hole?

In other words, create an adventure for them to follow. Take them on a chase, but avoid wild gooses. They run around with very little direction, unsure of where they are going or what they will do.

You begin with a little taste in the opening (frosting), a nibble in the Introduction (cupcake top), sprinkle throughout the message (cream filled cupcake), and offer a sample in the conclusion (sweet foundation).

Hungry?

What do you want listeners to know, think, and feel in order to follow through on the message? What do you want them to learn, how do you want them to think about it, and why should they feel anything at all? Is it enough that they should care because you think they should or simply because you said so?

Finally, when someone asks you what you are talking about, they are asking you for more than the subject of the speech. They want to understand your focus, intent, and the 5W&H of your presentation.

When you have these aspects decided, planning your speech is easier and you will own the stage with more verve than you ever imagined.

Final Words

Planning a speech or presentation can feel almost impossible, but with these tips, you will feel better prepared and more confident when meeting new faces standing in front of a podium, holding a mic, and voice the first syllable, remembering “I got this!”

Thank you for reading.

If you found these tips and quips helpful,
please post a review on Amazon.

Be well ☺

www.ingramcontent.com/pod-product-compliance
Ingram Content Group UK Ltd.
Pitfield, Milton Keynes, MK11 3LW, UK
UKHW020137250726
13967UKWH00002B/700

9 781523 295807